AF411849

# A Guidebook for Problem Solving in Group Settings

J. Gordon Myers, S.J.

John W. Lawyer

Sheed & Ward

Photocredits
Mimi Forsyth 8, 36
Cleo Freelance 24
John Glaser 26, 30



Sheed and Ward™ is a service of National Catholic Reporter Publishing, Inc.

ISBN: 0-934134-62-6

Published by:  Sheed and Ward
               115 E. Armour Blvd., P.O. Box 281
               Kansas City, MO 64141-0281

To order, call: 800-821-7926

**Dedication**

This guidebook is dedicated to our mothers, Catherine Lawyer and Dorothy Myers, who, among problem solvers stand preeminent. Their wit and wisdom, and love and care, continue to shape our lives.

# Contents

# OVERVIEW

Problem solving is a process of identifying a discrepancy between a current and a desired state and working out the steps required to reach that desired state. In the context of this book, problem solving is a process that enables a group to find a solution to a problem or difficulty. The problem can belong to the group as a whole or to any particular member of the group. In the latter case, the other members of the group become resource persons for ideas.

Not all problems call for the use of problem-solving skills; certain problems call only for the use of reflective listening skills. The skills used to help a group, or person in a group, will depend on correctly identifying the type of problem involved. The three types of problems that might be encountered are:

1. A problem that has no solution (for example, the death of a group member). Using reflective listening skills, you can provide a caring presence to the group or one or more of its members with this type of problem. By listening acceptingly and supportively, you allow the others to explore and express the emotions they are experiencing.

2. A problem or need that the group or one or more of its members has correctly identified and for which a solution is possible. Using reflective listening skills you can commit to be with the group's members as they explain the need or problem. In talking the matter through, they often clarify the need or problem and are thereby helped to discover and move toward a solution.

3. A problem or need that the group or one or more of its members has correctly identified and for which a solution is possible. In this case, however, the group or one or more of its members is "stuck" (unable to resolve the matter). The use of the problem-solving process presented in this book can facilitate finding or developing an appropriate solution to a problem.

Given that a problem is a discrepancy between the current state and a desired future state, it is useful in problem solving to express the problem in terms of the desired future state, or result. This can be done by wording the problem as a "How to ______" statement, using the following formula:

How to ________________________ ________________________ .
                (action verb)                 (desired result)

Example:

How to ________enhance________ __communication in our group__ .
                (action verb)                 (desired result)

How to ________motivate________ __for social justice in the parish__ .
                (action verb)                 (desired result)

Sometimes the interests or needs of a group or one or more of its members are ambiguous, vague, or global. When this occurs, we can use the following problem clarification process:

## Problem Interview*

1. Explore "problem as presented."

2. Paraphrase "problem as presented" as a "how to ______" statement.

3. Invite the appropriate group member(s) to share the history of the problem.

4. Ask the appropriate group member(s) to share what has been thought of or tried so far.

5. Invite the appropriate group member(s) to identify a desired result or wished for outcome.

6. Revisit "problem as presented" and modify it as appropriate.

7. Move to problem solving, if appropriate.


We can invite either the appropriate group member(s) or the group as a whole to use the seven-step, problem-solving process in either of two ways:

*The person asks for help —*

> We can say: "I'd be glad to help look at some options."

*You sense the person wants help —*

> We can ask: "Would you like us to help you look at some options?"

If the person indicates a positive response, describe the problem-solving process in one sentence, as follows:

A process that has been useful to me is to first identify the need, generate as many options as possible and, if one seems to make sense, work out a plan to make it happen. How does that sound for you?

The following figure illustrates how to enter the problem solving-process, utilizing problem clarification as required.


*Synectics, Inc.* (Programs in Creative Problem Solving), 26 Church Street, Cambridge, MA 02138.

Figure A.   Entering the Problem-Solving Process.


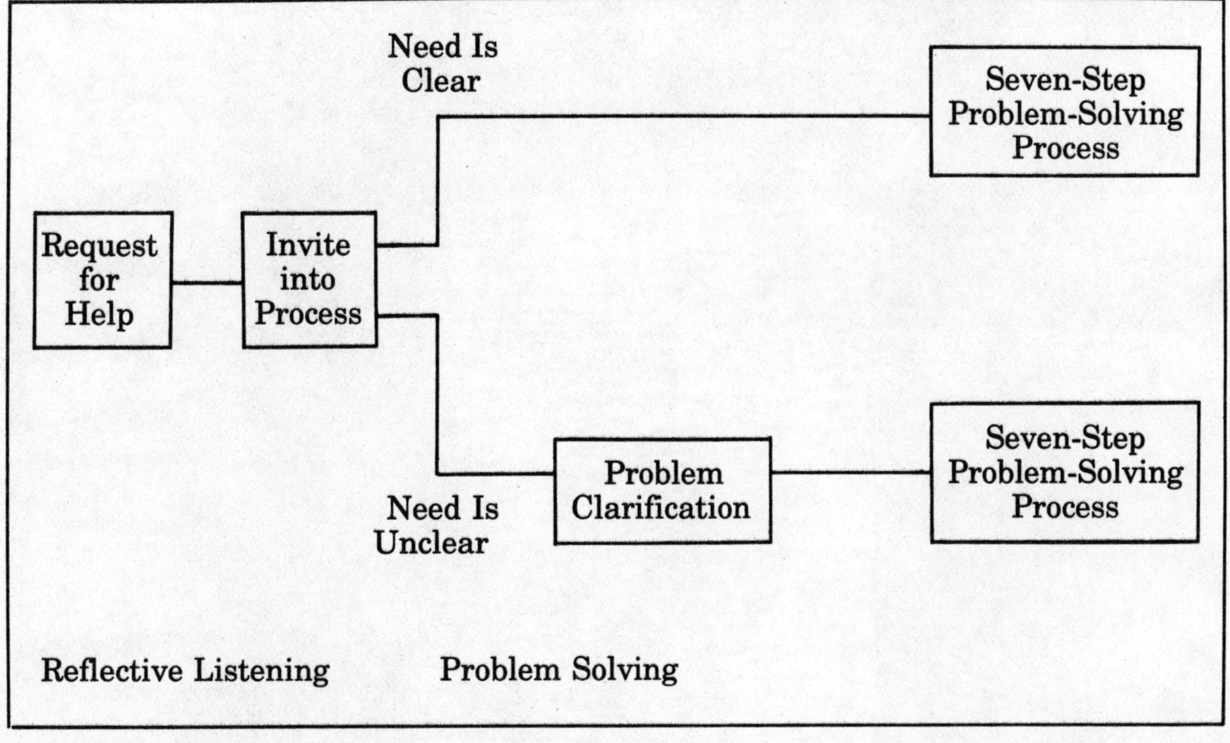

Need Is
Clear
Seven-Step
Problem-Solving
Process
Request
for
Help
Invite
into
Process
Problem
Clarification
Seven-Step
Problem-Solving
Process
Need Is
Unclear
Reflective Listening
Problem Solving

# INTRODUCTION

This book is intended to facilitate the problem-solving process. It outlines a process for problem solving in a group setting. It is designed to acquaint you with a specific problem-solving approach and assist you in working toward effective action on a concrete problem real to you.

The process involves seven steps:

1. Identifying and defining the problem.
2. Generating possible alternative solutions.
3. Evaluating the alternative solutions.
4. Deciding on the best acceptable solution.
5. Developing a plan of implementation for the solution.
6. Establishing a time and place for evaluation.
7. Reflecting on the group's collaborative effort.

After completing each step, but before moving on to the next one, critique your work.

Two additional steps are involved in problem solving using this method:

8. Implementing the solution.
9. Evaluating results.

These steps involve executing the plan developed and are not considered in this guidebook.

# Initial Organization of Work Group

At the outset, choose a facilitator whose task it is to remind the group of the guidelines and potential traps for each step of the process as that step emerges. The facilitator should also record the various responses made as the group moves through the seven-step problem-solving process.

## Suggested Procedure

1. Read through the seven steps which follow.
2. Remember the time limits within which you are working.
3. Complete the process with the specific problem.

# STEP 1: IDENTIFYING AND DEFINING THE PROBLEM

A problem is a discrepancy between the current situation and the desired situation:

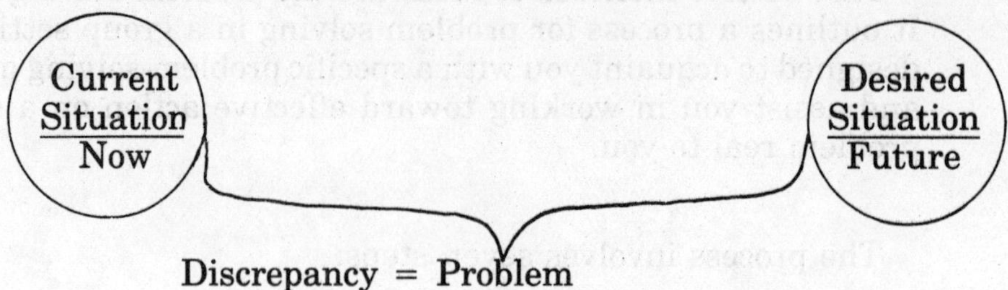


A. State the problem clearly and concisely. Make it as concrete and specific as possible.

B. Restate the problem in terms of the needs or interests of the person, group, or organization.

> For example:   The *problem* is how to sustain member-
> ship in our volunteer social service group.
>
> One possible need for the organization is how
> to support one another more effectively.

C. The facilitator gains acceptance of the need or interest statement from everyone in the work group, and writes it on *Worksheet A,* (which follows) beginning the statement with "How to . . . ."

> For example:   How to enable volunteers in the social
> service group to support one another effec-
> tively.

D. To gain further clarity on the need or interest statement, the group may choose to clarify the problem using the *Problem Interview* format discussed earlier in this book by briefly discussing the history of the "need," what has been thought of and/or tried so far, and any ideal wishes that group members may have for the organization. Should the group make this choice, *Worksheet A* can be used to record the group's work. A space is provided at the bottom of the worksheet for entering a more precise statement of the problem.

E. Check your problem statement for the following traps:
1. You've stated and, therefore, eventually will solve the wrong problem.
2. You've defined the problem in terms of a proposed solution, not a desired result.
3. You've not dug deeply enough. You've diagnosed the problem in terms of its symptoms, not the needs and interests of the parties.

F. When you have clearly and concretely defined the problem in terms of needs and interests, and examined it for traps go on to Step 2.

<u>Worksheet A — Identifying and Defining the Problem</u>

**Statement of Problem (Need or Interest)**
**"How to . . ."**

Clarification

**History of Problem**

**What Has Been Thought of or Tried So Far**

**Ideal Wish**

**Revised Statement of Problem (Need or Interest)**
**"How to . . ."**

## STEP 2:  GENERATING POSSIBLE ALTERNATIVE SOLUTIONS

A.  The key in this step is to generate a variety of solutions or options for solving the problem. This step is intended to encourage group members to offer suggestions without fear of rejection or a negative evaluation of their ideas. Group members are urged to offer as many suggestions as come to mind.

B.  This is a time to suspend critical judgment:

Brainstorm . . . . Nobody says "no."
Brainstorm . . . . Nobody says "that will never work."
Brainstorm . . . . Nobody says "that is a *dumb* idea."
Brainstorm . . . . Nobody says "that has already been tried."

C.  Before announcing possible solutions, each group member records his/her solutions or options on separate paper.

D.  When ready, the facilitator records the group members' solutions or options on *Worksheet B,* beginning with each member giving his or her two best. Second and third rounds may follow until the group members are satisfied that all possible solutions have been recorded.

E.  When the recording period is completed and the brainstorm session seems to have come to an end, work for a clearer understanding of the suggestions that have been made. Use inquiry — paraphrasing, seek clarification, offer examples or images, etc.

F.  Continue to suspend critical judgment until after this clarification period is completed.

G.  Avoid the trap of evaluating possible ideas and solutions as they are suggested.

Suggested Solutions or Options for Consideration:

## STEP 3:   EVALUATING THE ALTERNATIVE SOLUTIONS

A. In this step critical judgment is important.

B. Your group's brainstorm session has raised for consideration a range of possible solutions or options. Inquiry has clarified these.

C. Now you are ready to discuss these suggestions in order to select those which your group will decide upon for action.

D. Eliminate the suggestions which might obviously be inappropriate.

E. Narrow down the solutions to just three or four. Evaluate the suggestions and ideas that have been offered — feasibility, timing, expense, human resources, acceptability.

F. Put the remaining solutions in order of priority. You may say, "All right, which of these solutions look best?" or "Are any of these better than the others?"

G. Remember to be open and honest in stating your thoughts and feelings about those solutions that you simply think would not be useful at this time.

H. The facilitator lists on *Worksheet C* the group's top four possible or preferred solutions.

I. If an acceptable solution fails to emerge:

1. The group may choose to lower its aspirations so that a previously unacceptable solution now seems appropriate.
2. The group may take a break and then continue the search.
3. The group may modify or combine various solutions.

## Possible and Preferred Solutions

## STEP 4:   DECIDING ON THE MOST ACCEPTABLE SOLUTION

A.  By the time this step is completed, a clearly superior solution or option often emerges naturally from the discussion. The soluttion often involves a combination of the solutions or options identified in the brainstorming process. This step involves selecting the most creative — and best — solution that all parties find acceptable.

B.  Some tips for arriving at a final decision are:

1.  Keep testing out the remaining solutions against the feelings of the members of the group: "Are we all satisfied with this solution?"
2.  Don't think of a decision as necessarily final and impossible to change: "We seem to agree on this solution — let's start carrying it out and see if it really solves our problem and meets our needs."
3.  The facilitator writes down the solution and all of its parts, if it should contain several points, on *Worksheet D*.

<u>Worksheet D — Solution</u>

Solution Description (All Steps Involved)

## STEP 5: DEVELOPING A PLAN OF IMPLEMENTATION FOR SOLUTION

A. In this step the participants address themselves to such questions as: "Who is to do what by when."

B. Decide which person or persons should act on the ideas and plans.

C. Formulate the most acceptable solution arrived at in *Step 4* into concrete steps for action.

D. Remember to be concrete and specific. Action plans which are filled with vague generalizations are not useful.

E. Insure proper understanding of what needs to be done.

F. Insure acceptance and/or motivation for what needs to be done.

G. Provide appropriate resources (time, human resources, information, money) for what needs to be done.

H. The facilitator then records the full action plan on *Worksheet E*.

<u>Worksheet E — Action Plan</u>

| Step No. | Specific Steps | Person Responsible | Target Date |
|---|---|---|---|
|  |  |  |  |

**Additional Comments:**

19

The following steps are usually taken when the status of a problem is reviewed at a group meeting (Figure 2):

## STEP 6: ESTABLISHING A TIME AND PLACE FOR EVALUATION

A. Some action plans do not stand the test of time either in total or in part. Therefore, it is important to establish a process and date for evaluation. "Are we still satisfied with our action plan?" "Is there any part of it which needs reworking?" "In light of new data received, which changes now seem to be in order?"

B. "Who should do the evaluating?" and "How should it be done?"

C. "When do we suggest evaluating the results?"

D. Avoid the trap of failing to develop contingency plans in advance for anticipated problems.

E. The facilitator records the evaluative procedure on *Worksheet F* or adds a step to the action plan on *Worksheet E,* as appropriate.

Evaluation Plan:

| Step No. | Description | Person Responsible | Target Date |
|---|---|---|---|
| | | | |

## STEP 7:  REFLECTING ON GROUP'S
### COLLABORATIVE EFFORT

Your group has been working on a task — problem analysis and action planning. While working on the task, you need to look explicitly at both the problem-solving process and the interpersonal dimensions of your collaborative effort.

In terms of the interpersonal dimension, the deeply personal and human feelings of being prized or ignored, influential or not, can and must be understood in order to increase the probability of success in a group problem-solving situation. If these needs are not met, creativity is stifled and the problem-solving process loses much of the energy and creativity that might otherwise be available.

A.  Avoid the trap of working on a group task as if you can overlook the interpersonal dimensions and still produce good results from your group effort. Avoiding this trap can insure a more effective and efficient collaborative effort.

B.  Complete *Worksheet G* and discuss your reflections.

C.  Read *Worksheet H* and then discuss your reflections with the other group members.

D.  The facilitator now collects all the worksheets for a record of the group's proceedings.

**Worksheet G — Post-Meeting Reaction**

---

Fill in this sheet individually. Then read Worksheet H before discussing it with your group members. You will be asked to share what you write with the others.

---

1. How would you rate our cooperative effort? (*check one*)

   _____ poor   _____ mediocre   _____ all right   _____ good   _____ excellent

---

2. | What I said was being ignored |————————————————| What I said was prized and valued |

   (*circle a number*)

   1   2   3   4   5   6

---

3. What I liked best about our work together was . . .




---

4. If we could do the problem solving over again, a change I'd make is . . .

<u>Worksheet H</u>

*After reading this page, talk about your rating.*

Helpful

You will tend to be helpful when you are specific (i.e., "I felt prized by you, John, because often you asked me to say more when I spoke," *or* "an example of when I thought we fell into a trap was . . ." *or* "I felt put down when you . . .").

Not Helpful

You will tend to be judgmental and not helpful if you are general and evaluative (i.e., "You're the kind of person who puts people down," *or* "This group isn't working as well as it should be," *or* "I'm not having a good time").

Now, discuss your ratings — Be sure to use specific examples.

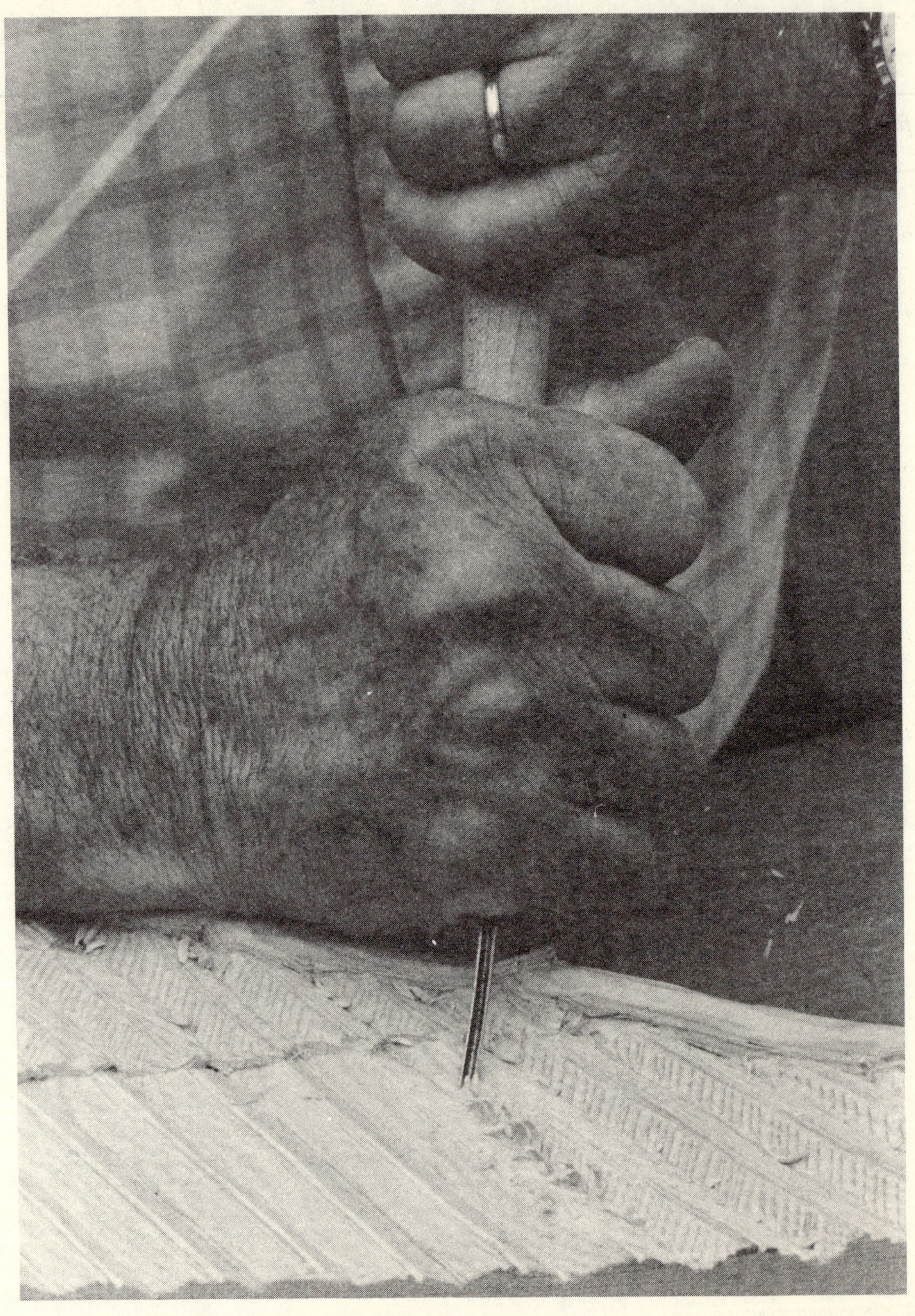

# PROBLEM MANAGEMENT

Problem management is a process that enables a group to identify and manage its problems as they occur in the life of the group. The process requires that the group meets regularly to identify problem areas, define specific problems, appoint a problem manager, develop tentative action plans, assign the next step to a specific individual, and specify a target date for completion.

The *Problem Management Worksheet* is a useful tool to help make this process work. The worksheet operates as a control for the problems. Problems are added to the current page of the worksheet as they are identified, with the next step carefully defined. When that step is completed a line is drawn through that item and the problem is reentered with the next step defined. When the last step is completed the problem is not reentered.

The *Problem Management Worksheet* pages with open items are duplicated and distributed to the group members prior to their regular meeting. The sheets become the agenda for the meeting. The meeting is conducted even though a group member(s) may be absent.

The sequence of events for identifying a problem and entering it into the problem management process is shown in Figure 1. Problems are reviewed at the group meeting following the target date for the current action step. The sequence of events for reviewing a problem's status are shown in Figure 2. A sample page from a *Problem Management Worksheet* is shown in Figure 3. A blank *Problem Management Worksheet* is shown in Figure 4.

The following steps are usually taken when a problem is identified (Figure 1):

1. The problem area is raised to the attention of the group by a group member (problem originator).

2. The problem is defined using a "how to . . ." statement.

3. A problem manager is assigned who is the keeper of the action plan and this is the person who manages the problem throughout its life.

4. An action plan is developed for the problem. (This is done either during the meeting, or subsequent to the meeting, by the problem manager.)

5. Problem manager presents action plan and responds to questions for clarification and gains agreement from the group members.

6. The next step to be taken with the problem is to identify it, assign it to a group member, and specify a target date (person responsible).

7. The problem and the next step are entered on the *Problem Management Worksheet* along with all the appropriate details (recorder).

The following steps are usually taken when the status of a problem is reviewed at a group meeting (Figure 2):

1. The problem manager presents the status of the problem, indicating what has happened to date with the current open-action step. If the action plan has not been agreed to by the group, the problem manager presents it to the group and negotiates agreement.

2. The problem manager facilitates group agreement of the next step, insuring that the person responsible for the next step is clear about what is to be done and by when.

3. The problem and the next step are entered on the *Problem Management Worksheet,* along with the appropriate details (recorder).

A three-ring notebook should be maintained by each group member with a section for the *Problem Management Worksheets* and a section for the action plans. The problem manager is responsible for controlling the problem and coordinating all efforts toward its solution. The action plan should be distributed to each person in the group after it is developed.

| Sequence of Events — Entering a New Problem | | | | | |
|---|---|---|---|---|---|
| Problem Originator | Group as Whole | Group Leader | Problem Manager | Group Recorder/ Secretary | Person Responsible |
| 0 identifies problem | | | | | |
| 0 presents tentative statement to group at meeting | | | | | |
| | 0 discusses problem and agrees on desirability and priority of need | | | | |
| | | 0 assigns problem manager in collaboration with group | | | |
| | | 0 sets target date in collaboration with group | | | |
| | | | 0 identifies first step and target date (the first step with a new problem is always "develop action plan") | | |
| | | | | 0 records problem statement, date entered, problem number, problem originator, problem manager, and target date as well as details of the first step (step number, action step, person responsible, and target date) | |
| | | | develops action plan for problem | | |
| | | | 0 gets agreement on action plan at next meeting | | |
| | | | | | 0 undertakes action step |

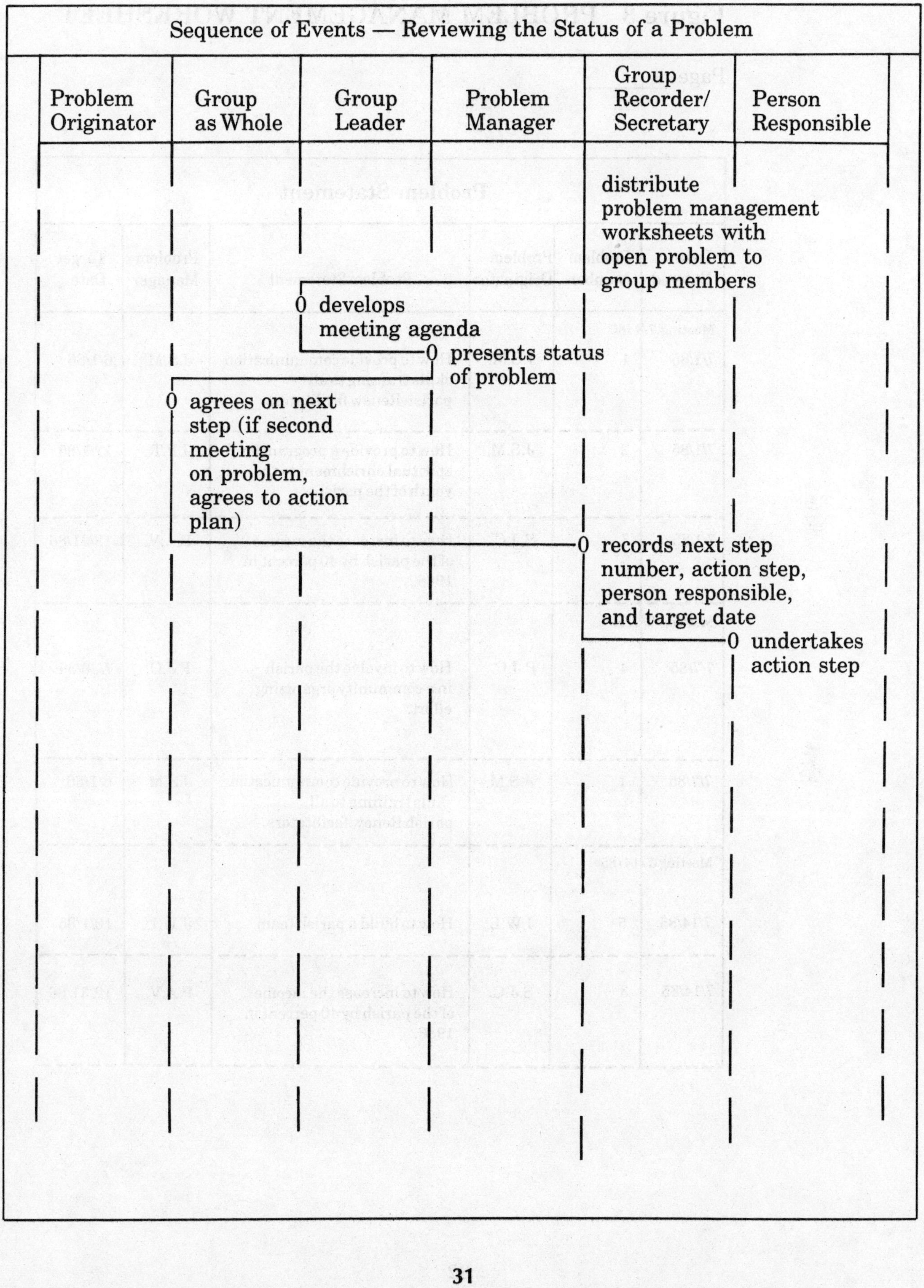

**Sequence of Events — Reviewing the Status of a Problem**

| Problem Originator | Group as Whole | Group Leader | Problem Manager | Group Recorder/ Secretary | Person Responsible |
|---|---|---|---|---|---|
| | | | | distribute problem management worksheets with open problem to group members | |
| | | 0 develops meeting agenda | | | |
| | | | 0 presents status of problem | | |
| | 0 agrees on next step (if second meeting on problem, agrees to action plan) | | | | |
| | | | | 0 records next step number, action step, person responsible, and target date | |
| | | | | | 0 undertakes action step |

# Figure 3   PROBLEM MANAGEMENT WORKSHEET

Page _______

| Problem Statement | | | | | |
|---|---|---|---|---|---|
| Date Entered | Problem Number | Problem Originator | Problem Statement | Problem Manager | Target Date |
| **Meeting 7/1/85** | | | | | |
| 7/1/85 | 1 | J.S.M. | How to provide communication skills training to all parish Renew facilitators. | J.S.M. | 6/1/86 |
| 7/1/85 | 2 | J.S.M. | How to provide a program for spiritual enrichment to the youth of the parish. | J.P.T. | 11/1/85 |
| 7/1/85 | 3 | S.J.C. | How to increase the income of the parish by 40 percent in 1986. | P.A.V. | 12/31/86 |
| **Meeting 7/7/85** | | | | | |
| 7/7/85 | 4 | P.J.C. | How to involve the parish in a community organizing effort. | P.J.C. | 7/30/86 |
| 7/7/85 | 1 | J.S.M. | How to provide communication skills training to all parish Renew facilitators. | J.S.M. | 6/1/86 |
| **Meeting 7/14/85** | | | | | |
| 7/14/85 | 5 | J.W.L. | How to build a parish team. | J.W.L. | 10/1/85 |
| 7/14/85 | 3 | S.J.C. | How to increase the income of the parish by 40 percent in 1986. | P.A.V. | 12/31/86 |

| Next Step | | | | |
|---|---|---|---|---|
| Step Number | Action Step | Person Responsible | Target Date | Completion Date |
| 1 | Develop action plan. Use Problem Solving Guidebook. | J.S.M | 7/7/85 | |
| 1 | Develop action plan. Use Problem Solving Guidebook. | S.P.C. | 8/15/85 | |
| 1 | Develop action plan. Use Problem Solving Guidebook. | P.A.V. | 7/14/85 | |
| 1 | Put together reading bibliography on community organizing for parish staff and parish council. | P.J.C. | 8/1/85 | |
| 2 | Retain consultant/trainer. | J.S.M. | 8/15/85 | |
| 1 | Develop action plan. Use Guidebook. | J.W.L. | 8/15/85 | |
| 2 | Put together a sacrificial giving team. | P.A.V. | 8/15/85 | |

# Figure 4  PROBLEM MANAGEMENT WORKSHEET

Page _______

| | | | Problem Statement | | |
|---|---|---|---|---|---|
| Date Entered | Problem Number | Problem Originator | Problem Statement | Problem Manager | Target Date |
| | | | | | |

| Step Number | Action Step | Person Responsible | Target Date | Completion Date |
|---|---|---|---|---|
| | | | | |

# ANNOTATED BIBLIOGRAPHY

Gordon, Thomas. *Leadership Effectiveness Training.* New York:
Wyden, 1977. Offers an excellent model and method for problem solving useful to those responsible for the leadership of
a variety of organizations.

Huber, George P. *Managerial Decision Making.* Glenview, Illinois:
Scott, Foresman and Company, 1980. Divided into three
parts, (1) Overview of decision making and problem solving;
(2) Individual decision making; and (3) Group decision making. This book applies contemporary research, theory, and
techniques to very universal leadership dilemmas.

Toner, Jules. "Method for Communal Discernment of God's Will,"
Vol. III, no. 3 (June, 1971), *Studies in the Spirituality of
Jesuits,* The American Assistancy Seminar, Fusz Memorial,
3700 West Pine Blvd., St. Louis, Missouri, 63108 (approx.
$1.00). This monograph sets forth a practical method for in-
corporating prayer and the discernment of Spirits into the
process of communal or group decision making. Very clearly
written, this pamphlet integrates well with the seven-step
method presented in this resource volume.

Whitehead, Evelyn E., and James D. *Method in Ministry, Theological Reflection and Christian Ministry,* New York: The Sea-
bury Press, 1980. Presents a proven method and a practical
model for theological reflection for the sake of making effective
pastoral choices in a small or large group setting. More than
any other source, this book provides the best theological
foundation to support the problem-solving process presented
in this manual.